BILLERICAY

An Historical Tour in Pictures

including
South Green, Crays Hill,
Ramsden Heath, Ramsden Bellhouse and
Little and Great Burstead

BILLERICAY

An Historical Tour in Pictures

including
South Green, Crays Hill,
Ramsden Heath, Ramsden Bellhouse and
Little and Great Burstead

Roger Green

Phillimore

1997

Published by
PHILLIMORE & CO. LTD.
Shopwyke Manor Barn, Chichester, West Sussex

ISBN 1 86077 067 3

Printed and bound in Great Britain by
BUTLER AND TANNER LTD.
London and Frome

The Tour

Preface and Acknowledgements

One Sunday morning in 1991 I was driving along the Stock Road towards Billericay and as I passed the Mayflower County High School I observed a large banner displayed at the entrance ' Postcard Fair Here Today'. Turning the car around was the first act in something that has monopolised the majority of my free time since then. That day I purchased six postcards of Billericay, the first of the hundreds to follow. This book is the result of six years' travelling to postcard fairs around the country searching for elusive postcards and pictures of Billericay past. It is designed as a 'tour' which starts at the Stock side of Billericay, encompassing the entire High Street, including all the side roads, through the villages of Little and Great Burstead, followed by South Green, Crays Hill, Ramsden Bellhouse and Ramsden Heath, and then returning to Billericay.

Ninety-five per cent of the pictures in this book are from my own collection, but without the willingness of others to allow pictures and postcards from their own collections to be printed, then the 'tour' of Billericay would not have been complete. In this regard, I would specially like to thank Peter Storey, Peter Murray, Michael Shelley, Joyce Norris, Mrs. M. Mayger, A.M. Jackson, A.J. Whitworth, Mrs. G.M.West, Mrs. Mander and Terry Strong for allowing me access to their collections. Illustrations on pages 29 (bottom), 33 (top) and 55 (top) are reproduced by courtesy of the Essex Record Office. As there must be many pictures relating to Billericay that lie in private photo albums and private collections I encourage the owners of them to contact me as work on the second volume on Billericay is already in hand.

I finally acknowledge the patience of my family for the disarray I imposed and especially my daughter Sophie who personally assisted me in searching through literally tens of thousands of postcards to discover the pictorial history of Billericay.

ROGER GREEN

Introduction

Billericay, in the county of Essex, lies 25 miles to the east of London. It is a town of historic interest, rich in 16th-to18th-century properties which have been carefully preserved through the centuries. English history touches the town with a Bronze-Age settlement, Roman invasion, the massacre of the Battle of Billericay, the martyrs who chose death rather than renouncing their faith, the hope of the Billericay pioneers who sailed with the Pilgrim Fathers on the *Mayflower* to America and the excitement of the Zeppelin crash during the First World War.

Billericay's broad High Street is some 315 ft. above sea level and 830 yards long. It is virtually unchanged in layout during the last 500 years. To the north is the city of Chelmsford, to the east Wickford, to the south the new town of Basildon and to the west lies Brentwood. Within the surrounding countryside are the villages of Little and Great Burstead, South Green, Crays Hill, Ramsden Bellhouse and Ramsden Heath.

Billericay is built on a ridge of well-drained Bagshot sands and there is still evidence today of the many wells and water pumps that existed in Billericay High Street. With an abundant supply of water it is understandable that this ridge was chosen for settlement.

It is hard to imagine what Billericay was like in those early days. The surrounding area of heavy clay would have been covered with woodland with the High Street ridge being heathland. From the top of the ridge, looking towards the Thames, was one vast forest as far as the eye could see. The view is still there today but only through gaps between the buildings.

To the east of the High Street is Norsey Woods, where evidence of Bronze-Age occupation has been discovered. There are two burial mounds where cremated remains were uncovered, revealing that the deceased's ashes were accompanied by his or her possessions placed in earthenware urns. From this time very little is known until the Iron Age.

Following three waves of Celtic migration into Essex from Europe, in the period 500-100 B.C., the Romans invaded twice in 55 and 54 B.C. At the time of Julius Caesar's invasion, the Billericay area was occupied by the Trinovantes, who, in addition to being farmers, were fighters and defenders of their territory. They lived in large, thatched circulated buildings with an opening in the roof for smoke. The buildings were made of wattle and daub, a form of construction consisting of interwoven twigs plastered with a mixture of clay, lime, water and sometimes dung and chopped straw.

One can only guess that there were probably only a dozen families living in farmsteads containing three generations, but consisting of a sound tribal organisation. Caesar conquered the Trinovantes, as did the final Roman invasion in A.D. 43 under the Roman Emperor Claudius. It was that invasion that saw elephants in Colchester and all Southern England from the Wash to the Severn under Roman rule.

In time, the Trinovantes became friendly with the Romans and their wealthy chieftains adopted the Roman way of life. However, despite this, they were not well treated. When through mistreatment Queen Boudicca of the Iceni tribe in Norfolk rose against the Romans in A.D. 61 her armies were joined by the Trinovantes.

Queen Boudicca destroyed the Roman towns of Colchester, St Albans and London and slaughtered the inhabitants. There is no evidence of any fighting in the Billericay area and it must be presumed that Boudicca bypassed the town, which was by then an established Roman settlement, on her way to London. (She was eventually killed in battle by the armies of the Roman general Suetonius Paulinus. This defeat was followed by severe reprisals over the whole area.)

That Billericay was definitely a Roman settlement is proved by the evidence discovered through excavations throughout the area including the High Street, Norsey Wood, Outwood Common Road, Perry Street and at the

Billericay School site. These have yielded coins (covering the first to fourth centuries), bricks, pottery, brooches, and numerous artifacts, many of which are in the possession of the Billericay Archaeological and Historic Society at their headquarters in Sun Street, Billericay.

The small Roman force, which was encamped on the high ground in Billericay, had a stronghold in an arc that stretched from near the site of St Mary Magdalen Church in the High Street to above Norsey Wood. This position provided a defensive view over the entire surrounding forests. Later, an additional outpost was built at Blunts Wall, which is near Tye Common and west of the High Street. Although it is believed that this was a Roman fort there have been doubts as to the purpose of the buildings constructed there. Roman burial places have been discovered in Norsey Woods and in the burial ground in Chapel Street. Stone coffins, which appeared to be from the Roman periods, were discovered in the 18th century and replaced.

A.D. 410 marked the end of the Roman occupation, when the Roman troops were recalled to Rome. By this time Britain had been part of the Roman empire for 400 years and the occupied areas were instructed to defend themselves, against the Scots (Picts) from the north, the Irish (via Wales) from the west or the Saxons, who had been attacking the east coast of England for decades. In the years following A.D. 410 waves of Saxons attacked and invaded until Britain fell under their rule. Essex was the East Saxons' kingdom, as Norfolk was North Folk, and Suffolk was South Folk.

The earliest records indicate that in A.D. 600 England was divided into kingdoms, and Billericay was within the kingdom of Essex. The Saxons eventually settled in the area, not on the Billericay ridge but at Great Burstead. Known in 1086 as Burghsteda, the name 'burgh' means 'fortified place, place of strategic value'; the word 'steda' means 'farmstead, place where people live', which suggests that Great Burstead was a fortified settlement with a market and its own civil administration.

There is no proof that Great Burstead was the actual seat of the kings of Essex, but it grew to become one of the more important villages in the area whilst at that time the Billericay ridge was probably uninhabited. The importance of Great Burstead lasted until the 19th century, when Billericay was part of the parish of Great Burstead. In due course the town of Billericay grew and became the commercial centre, but the ecclesiastical control remained at Great Burstead.

Between the years A.D. 900 and 1000 England saw the creation of hundreds, units of justice and administration; Billericay was within the Barstable hundred. In those days the average person would not travel beyond his hundred, and unless he went to war he would spend his whole life in the same village. By this time the forest was being cut down for fuel and to make way for agricultural land.

In A.D. 1066 William the Conqueror ascended the throne of England after defeating Harold at Hastings. In 1086 he wanted precise details of all land holdings together with stock numbers throughout the country, and a general survey was conducted to record the number of people, their lands, and details of their stock. All this information was collated and entered in Domesday Book.

The name of Billericay does not appear in Domesday Book. In 1066 there were only a few houses along the Billericay ridge and at that time they were not part of Great Burstead. However, between the years 1066 and 1086 Billericay was annexed to Great Burstead, and the Survey gives the first indication of the population of Billericay at the time of William the Conqueror.

For Great Burstead, in 1066, the survey records one manor, 12 ploughs, 20 villagers (villeins), five smallholders (boarders), half a hide of woodland and pasture for 150 sheep, two cobs (riding horses), 11 cattle, 106 pigs, 219 sheep, the total of which was worth £20. After 1066, the area of Billericay was added to Great Burstead which then contained 28 freeman holding 28 hides and five acres, on which there were 16 ploughs, five hides of woodland (probably Norsey Woods), 23 acres of meadow and pasture for 250 sheep, 54 smallholders and four slaves. The size of families that made up the population of Billericay is unknown, but basing a calculation on four to a family, it must have been in the region of 350. Taking into account the number of freemen Billericay had, it must reflect on Billericay's commercial importance as compared to the smaller adjoining Great Burstead under whose jurisdiction it operated.

The lord of the manor at this time was Bishop Odo of Bayeux, half-brother of William the Conqueror. Following William's victory, Odo was rewarded with 216 lordships in the country, of which 39 (including Great Burstead) were in Essex. Following rebellious activity when he attempted to go to Rome with a vast fortune in order to try to become pope, Odo was arrested and banished from England; his lands (including Great Burstead, which by now had annexed Billericay) were confiscated and surrendered to the crown. Little Burstead, Crays Hill and Ramsden (Bellhouse and Crays) were all mentioned in Domesday Book. Little Burstead was then a manor of three hides (360 acres) with two villagers, one smallholder and six slaves; Crays Hill was part of a manor of two hides and 30 acres (270 acres in total); there are numerous entries for Ramsden in Domesday Book. South Green was not listed. The first record for South Green was by the Elizabethan mapmaker Ralph Agas, who named it 'Southwoode Greene'. The area was what the name suggested, a green that was used by the people for various activities.

No records exist until 1185 when there was a grant of the manor lands to the Stratford Abbey. Normally land, once given to the Church, remained with the Church, in exchange for saying mass for your soul. In 1253 King Henry III and in 1285 King Edward I granted Stratford Abbey the right to hold markets, but it is not known whether they were held in Billericay High Street or at Great Burstead. Certainly in the 16th century markets were held in the High Street, but the exact site of the 1253 market is unknown. Although logic says the 1253 market must have been in the commercial centre of town—along the Billericay ridge—it was probably held at Great Burstead. In the 1300s there are some references to Billericay in the records but they mention the roadway—the road to Tilbury via Billericay.

The name of Billericay did not appear in the market grant of 1253 and the first reference to its name was not found until 1291—Byllyrica. Over the years the recorded spelling of the name changed many times including, 1307 Billirica, 1343 Billerica and Beleuca, 1351 Byllerica, 1368 Billeryke, 1382 Bellerica, 1395 Billerica, 1436 Billyrecha, 1514 Belerikkey, 1539 Bulerycay, 1594 Billerecay, and in 1686 Bilreaky. The author in his research has discovered and now has possession of a 1627 map where the name is shown as Belericay. There is total mystery as to the origin of the name.

Around 1342/5 Billericay acquired a chantry chapel, when sufficient lands were given to support the living requirements of a priest. Religion played a significant role in everyday life and the teachings of the Church were accepted by the people without question.

For Billericay the church was at Great Burstead and townsfolk would have had to walk to attend compulsory services. If you lived on the west side of Billericay in Mountnessing parish you had to walk to Mountnessing church. This was arduous, especially in winter over unmade, rutted, muddy and frozen soil, and access to Mountnessing church was impossible when the river Wid was in flood. The townsfolk also had to pay tithes to the church; there was an agreement that the people on the west side of Billericay could pay their tithes to and attend Great Burstead church, but compensation had to be arranged for Mountnessing church to receive the tithe payments from elsewhere. The tithe payments were very important to the church as they normally represented a sum equal to one tenth of agricultural or other produce, personal income or profits of the payer.

All these problems were resolved with the establishment of a chantry/chapel of ease in Billericay that stood on the site of St Mary Magdalen Church in High Street. A chantry was usually a private chapel and prayers were said for individuals and members of their families who had previously paid for them. The original chapel was built on the site of the existing church and the chapel's lands were to the east of it. The priest would have lived in a building on the site of 57 to 61 High Street. The original chapel would have been built of oak; in approximately 1490 it was completely rebuilt in brick. Today the only part of the church that has survived from the 15th century is the tower, as the remaining part of the chapel was rebuilt in 1780.

All the tithe payments still had to be paid to the Great Burstead church, and the people of Billericay had to make extra payments for the upkeep of the High Street church. The chantry priest would have also had additional duties as a school teacher.

In 1551, under King Edward VI, the chantries were suppressed and the king sold the Billericay chantry to the Tyrell family who purchased not only the chantry but also its lands. The Tyrell family kept the lands and sold the chantry to the inhabitants of Billericay in trust for their use. Because it was not known whether the chantry was rightly consecrated, the trustees surrendered their rights to the Bishop of London on 30 August 1693 and the following 8 October he consecrated and dedicated it to St Mary Magdalen. It is not known to which patron saint the original chantry chapel was dedicated but there is evidence of a bequest in 1524 to the priest of St John's Chapel in Billericay. There is also a mystery in respect of an inscription on one of the bells of the Chantry: 'SANCTE KATRINA ORA PRO NOBIS' (St Katharine pray for us) when the church was dedicated to St Mary.

Discussion of the church has bypassed a very important event that affected Billericay in the 14th century. 1381 marked the Peasants' Revolt when Essex and Kent men protested against the introduction of Richard II's poll tax. The wars with France in the 14th century were a drain on the economy and the crown's resources, so the king's advisors were always trying to raise more money. There was considerable inflation after 1350 and by 1380 the king was desperate to raise money and did so by way of a poll tax on individuals. At that time the peasants were already dissatisfied with the amount of taxes they were paying and the poll tax brought everything to a head.

When the inspectors were sent out to collect the tax lists the people would not put their names down and tried to evade the tax. The revolt began at Brentwood and the King's Justice, Sir Robert Belknap, was sent to Brentwood to resolve matters. On 2 June 1387 he was met by a crowd of angry armed men from numerous parishes, including Billericay and, after several of his officers were killed, escaped with his life. The Essex men, the leader of whom was a weaver from Billericay, then proceeded to destroy the manor records and marched to London where the king rode out to meet them at Mile End. The next day, after joining forces with the men of Kent (led by Wat Tyler), they marched to Smithfield in London where the Lord Mayor of London stabbed and killed Wat Tyler. The king then made false promises to the crowd; only after returning home and realising the promises were worthless, did the Essex men assemble again.

They were hunted down by the king's forces and eventually fled to Billericay where they barricaded themselves in Norsey Wood behind the deerbank and wooden palisades. The army that chased them was led by Sir Thomas of Woodstock and Sir Thomas Percy who attacked the Essex men in Norsey Wood. The king's men were a trained fighting force wearing body armour, with knights fully equipped on horseback. The defenders were labourers armed with spades, forks and sticks, no match for the fighting machine that tore through them. The Battle of Billericay ended with the massacre of five hundred peasants whilst the remainder fled northwards. No bodies were ever found in the woods—it can be only assumed that they were removed and buried at Great Burstead Church. This is clear evidence that the people who lived in the Billericay area did not accept authority lightly nor, as will be shortly observed, be told what religion they should believe in. The Peasants' Revolt did not achieve a great deal and it left a certain amount of unease.

After the massacre in Norsey Wood the people of Billericay were easily influenced by the 'Lollards' (travelling priests, whose founder had translated the bible into English in 1378). The peasants had a desire to hear the bible read in English and bible reading groups were arranged for this to be achieved. The Church persecuted the Lollards and their followers for heresy; bible meetings therefore had to be held in secret and it was these meetings that gave birth to Puritan traditions in Billericay.

In the 15th century Billericay was prosperous. The population at that time was approximately 1,200 which, when compared with London (35,000), Norwich (6,000) and Winchester (2,000), gives an indication of the town's importance. It was a centre for the wool trade, employing woolmen and skinners, and it had its own tanneries. The King's Justices also held a court here. It is evidence of the success and importance of Billericay throughout the area that in 1476 King Edward IV confirmed and granted the right to hold a market and two fairs at Billericay.

Billericay was a stopping point for travellers, traders and pilgrims, especially those going to Tilbury to cross the Thames. With the development of the market and as a converging point of various routes, Billericay became the largest trading centre and market town within the Barstable hundred. Most villagers would have had to walk over unmade roads to the Tuesday markets and the two markets that were held on 22 July and 7 October each year. The centre of the market was the market house and the market cross which stood, together with the pillory and the stocks, at the Chapel Street/High Street junction. There were also at the corner a well and a pump for public use. Billericay became an increasingly important market town and expanded to accommodate the market's customers and travellers. By the late 1500s the High Street was fully developed.

The religious situation created total chaos and upheaval throughout the following decades. When Edward VI came to the throne in 1547 he took a Protestant stance and this religion was imposed during his reign. After his death, and following Mary's eventual coronation on 1 October 1553, she re-established and enforced the Roman Catholic religion. This obviously caused religious conflict to those with Protestant beliefs, who had to change to the Catholic religion. Many refused to change and as a result were burnt at the stake. Billericay had its martyrs: Thomas Watts, a linen draper, was burnt at Chelmsford in 1555; James Harris, who was only 17, was burnt at Smithfield, London, and Margaret Ellis, Joan Potter, Joan Horns, and Elizabeth Thackvel, four Billericay women, would not recant their Protestant beliefs. In 1556 Joan Horns, Elizabeth Thackvel (who were just teenagers) and Joan Potter were burnt at Smithfield, whilst Margaret Ellis died in Newgate prison whilst awaiting her fate.

It was hoped that these examples would persuade the rest of the community to conform. Queen Mary was wrong and her harsh punishments only had the reverse effect. Her reign of terror, in which a fourth of all martyrs came from Essex (they numbered 73), and the strength of those willing to die rather than abandon their beliefs, had the result of making Essex, including Billericay, the most Protestant county in England.

Elizabeth I followed and reigned until 1603. Billericay prospered during her reign; the countryside became safer for travellers and business for its inns increased. There was less persecution of Puritans during her reign, but everyone was required to attend church and a fine or imprisonment was enforced for failure to do so.

Following her death, James I was crowned king and once again problems arose which led to the *Mayflower* venture. In order to escape from persecution the Pilgrim Fathers set sail for the new world from Plymouth on 6 September 1620. Four Billericay inhabitants sailed with them, including Christopher Martyn who was governor of the ship. He was married to Marie Prowe and had his business in the High Street. Legend states that he lived at 57 to 61 High Street (which was originally one building) but there is no documentary proof to support this, although he did own property on the other side of the street. It is believed that the Essex contingent met at 57-61 High Street the night before they left to join the *Mayflower*. The journey to America was successfully completed but unfortunately the entire Billericay contingent died from illness during the first winter. Many from Essex traced their footsteps and, following a petition by Billericay emigrants, the new town of Billerica was established by the Massachusetts Legislature on 23 May 1655.

In Billericay problems for the Puritans continued until licensed meeting places for dissenters were permitted. There is a plaque affixed to 91 High Street stating that the Independent Protestant Dissenters first met there in 1672. In 1691, the Puritans smashed down the door of Billericay church, destroyed the fittings and removed the prayer books.

From 1642 to 1660 England was in the midst of civil war. The fighting did not affect Billericay until 1648 when Parliamentarian forces marched through Billericay to challenge the Royalist forces on 13 June at Colchester. The Great Plague of 1665 left Essex comparatively untouched although many must have fled towards Billericay from London to escape the illness.

In the 18th century, many older houses in Billericay were demolished to make way for fine Georgian properties, many of which are still in existence today. Billericay's importance as a coaching centre grew with road development. Three coaches a day would call at Billericay on their journeys between Southend and London, and that was in addition to the local traffic. Travelling by coach was not accident-free especially when highwaymen, like Essex-born Dick Turpin, were around. Turpin himself operated in this area of Essex and legend has it that, to escape his pursuers, he rode his horse up the staircase of the original *Crown Inn* in Billericay and jumped out of the top window.

Brickmaking, pottery, tile-making and the clothing trade became important local industries. The 'Ghastly Miller of Billericay' became known nationally for his slimming diet of flour sea biscuits and skimmed milk. During the Napoleonic Wars soldiers were billeted in the barracks in Sun Street.

In 1832 Billericay become a Parliamentary polling station, and in 1840 under the Poor Law legislation, the town became the centre of a Union of Parishes to help the poor. A union, otherwise known as a workhouse, was built in Billericay, now part of St Andrew's Hospital on Stock Road. A workhouse was primarily for families who could not support themselves, deserted spouses with their children, and widows. In 1844 Billericay was established as a separate ecclesiastical parish.

Although its population was rising, many results of the Industrial Revolution contributed to the start of the decline of Billericay's importance in the late 18th and early 19th centuries. The passing of wealth from the country towns to the new industrialised areas, the development of the new turnpike road system (which made travelling to other markets within the country much easier), the ability to travel further distances without the necessity of stopping overnight at one of Billericay's inns, and the bypassing of Billericay by the railway (until 40 years later when the railway reached Billericay in 1888) are just some.

The markets of Billericay, which had drawn such prosperity to the town for so many centuries, gradually declined until they finally ceased around the end of the 19th century. It was during this period of decline that many of the unemployed labourers of Billericay were involved in the manual work of creating Lake Meadows, now enjoyed by thousands of Billericay residents. With the arrival of goods trains in 1888 and the first passenger service on 1 January 1889 Billericay was given an opportunity to claw back some of its importance. This was accelerated with the gradual appearance of motor vehicles on the roads of Billericay in the early 1900s.

The decline is evidenced by the relevant entries in *Kelly's* directories of the era. *Kelly's Directory* of 1855 describes Billericay as a 'small market town and within the ecclesiastical district of the Parish of Great Burstead. It was part of the Hundred of Barstable and the head of a union of 24 people. The town has been much improved by the building of new houses and is lighted with gas and has a fine view of the Thames, the Nore and the coast of Kent in fine weather. Petty sessions are held once a fortnight in the Town Hall. Population in 1851 was 1533.' Great Burstead is described as 'a pleasant village & parish, lies a mile and a half to the south of Billericay. It formerly possessed a market. Contains 3,502 acres and a population of 722. Soil light & gray, chief crops wheat and barley.' Little Burstead was '2 miles to the south west containing 1829 acres, with the population in 1851 of 179'. The description in the 1870 edition of *Kelly's* contrasts sharply, when the town was described as 'a small decayed market town'.

At the beginning of the 20th century Billericay once again became a backwater, a small country town, a town where many had heard its name but could not place where it was. That was so until the night of 23/24 September 1916 during the First World War when Flight-Lieutenant Souray shot down an L-32 Zeppelin over the skies of Essex. The Zeppelin crashed from the skies to the east of the High Street in the fields off Jackson's Lane. Within hours hundreds of sightseers were on their way to observe the fallen Zeppelin, which by then was guarded and protected by hundreds of soldiers. Within days the whole of the country knew the whereabouts of Billericay. The entire crew of the craft were killed and their bodies buried at Great Burstead Church. The bodies were later exhumed and taken to the German war cemetery in Staffordshire. (This book contains some of the photographs taken that day.)

Billericay men were called to arms in both world wars and the war memorial stands at the corner of Chapel Street and High Street to mark their sacrifice. Buildings in Billericay were requisitioned by the army during the war and used for war purposes. Although it appears that there were no planned bombing raids on Billericay, the town was in the path of German bombers heading for and returning from London, and over a hundred bombs fell in the Billericay area. In September 1940 a land mine did fall towards the High Street, but fortunately an alert anti-aircraft crew, stationed in the lookout on top of (then) 39 High Street, managed to explode it before it landed Otherwise probably it would have probably flattened a large section of the High Street.

Since the two world wars Billericay has changed. However, it has retained many of its beautiful old buildings that have stood for some 400 to 500 years, though it is disappointing that more have not survived. This book is a record of that era, with photographs and postcards being used in preference to words.

Billericay, towards the end of the 20th century, is a busy Essex town trying to protect its inheritance, whilst at the same time coping with the ever expanding magnet of out-of-town and new town shopping centres. Its population has increased from some 350 in 1066, and 1,472 at the time of the first national census in 1801, to 35,000 today. The population is still expanding through new housing development and, with a commuter workforce, the station now has more trains per hour than it did per day at the start of the century. Billericay itself has many factories on its industrial estate and hundreds of businesses lining its High Street, including many companies who have decentralised from London.

Billericay does not have the facilities of the large adjoining towns, but it still has a population that supports its heart, being the High Street that still sits high up on the Billericay Ridge. It is known nationally through the television and media coverage of its successive Members of Parliament; it was traditionally the first constituency to declare a result at the general election. On 3 July 1996 it was thrust into the limelight through the murder of one of its traders, Julian Shone, who, when going about his daily tasks, was shot and murdered by armed raiders when he bravely tackled them. Throughout the 1990s' recession Billericay High Street did not reflect the emptiness and vacant look of many other towns—its shops were fully occupied, serving the town's customers in the way their ancestors have done through the century's past. Billericay still has its butcher, baker, fishmonger, tailor, coffee shop, bookseller, and many other small individual and independent businesses that comprise its backbone.

This very concise history does not even scratch the surface of Billericay past. Those who are interested in further reading should refer to the books and articles listed in the Bibliography, linking the same with a visit to the Cater Museum at 74 High Street, Billericay. Work has already commenced on a further book on Billericay and the author welcomes contact from anyone who has old photographs and postcards relating to the town, its surrounding area and activities that have occurred within those areas.

As one approached Billericay from the north along the Stock Road in the turnpike era, a compulsory stop would have been made at the toll keeper's house, which is the building on left. (This postcard was posted in Billericay on 6 July 1905.)

The 1912 picture (below) is of the opposite view and the toll house can been seen in the distance on the right of the road. Hill House Cottage is on the left and, as can be seen in the bottom left 1997 picture, it survives today. All the buildings on the right have been demolished and in their place stands the Health Centre site, which is part of the St Andrew's Hospital complex.

The right picture is taken just past Hill House Drive on the left and before Headley Road on the right. Date unknown but after the Second World War.

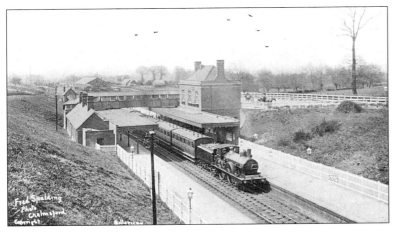

Construction of the railway line to Billericay commenced in 1884 with the first goods traffic running in 1888. The deepest cutting on the line to Billericay and Wickford was at Billericay (54 ft.), all the excavation being done by hand. The excavated soil was removed to outside the station and was used as a back drop for a target range during the First World War.

The first passenger steam train was the 7.30 a.m. from Wickford to Billericay on 1 January 1889. The first train from Liverpool Street to Billericay (such trains previously terminated at Brentwood) was the 10.15 a.m. on the same day. The railway bridge, viewing areas and the platform were crowded as the first train from London was welcomed by a band and a cheering crowd.

Electric trains replaced the steam trains, the chimney stacks of the station building were removed and the surrounding area was developed from open fields to a modern garage with the Billericay Industrial Estate beyond. Modern buses and cars replace the horse and trap awaiting the train passengers.

The photographer who took the picture above was standing with his back to the station entrance, facing east towards Stock Road. St Andrew's Hospital (formerly The Union, which was built in 1840 and used as a workhouse) is shown on the top left with Pear Tree Cottages on the far side of Stock Road.

The modern-day scene bears no resemblance to that of the late 1800s. The view to the hospital is blocked by the rear side of the Radford Way parade of shops. Pear Tree Cottages were demolished in 1935 to be replaced by a garage, itself replaced by a block of flats in the 1980s.

These two pictures are taken from the same location. The hand-operated signal box on the upside platform was demolished when the platform was lengthened. A large car park for commuters now exists where perishable goods used to be transported in the goods yard; the four rail tracks were reduced to two when the goods yard became redundant. The foliage in the modern picture completely obliterates the view of the surrounding area.

Past the railway station, down Radford Way, the entrance to Lake Meadows is on the right-hand side. The original swimming pool was on the far side and the site is now in the garden of one of the houses in Lakeside. Unlike today's modern pool, swimmers had mud, frogs and grass snakes for company as they swam. The white building was one of the changing rooms.

Two pictures (top right) of Gooseberry Green show Mountnessing Road with Perry Street to the right. Railway Cottages, which stood to the left of the white fence together with all the buildings shown, were demolished and replaced with a public house and a shopping parade. Prior to its demolition the house to the right of the picture became vacant, rundown and overgrown. It became known to the children of Billericay as the 'Witches House'. The dirt track is now a busy roundabout with the industrial estate situated on the opposite side. (The old postcard was posted on the 14 July 1913 in Billericay.)

Back-tracking up Radford Way is the railway bridge …

With the construction of the railway in 1884 came the railway bridge at the north end of the High Street. (The old postcard was posted on 25 April 1930.) The view of the workhouse is almost completely hidden with foliage with buildings appearing on the Stock Road. Mr. Iles' name, advertising his estate agency, can be seen on the roof line of his property. The carts crossing the bridge belong to Harris Bros., coal merchants, each cart being full of coal for sale. The 1997 photograph shows the scene some 70 years later, featuring modern flats built on the far side of the bridge and a metal pedestrian footbridge alongside the road bridge.

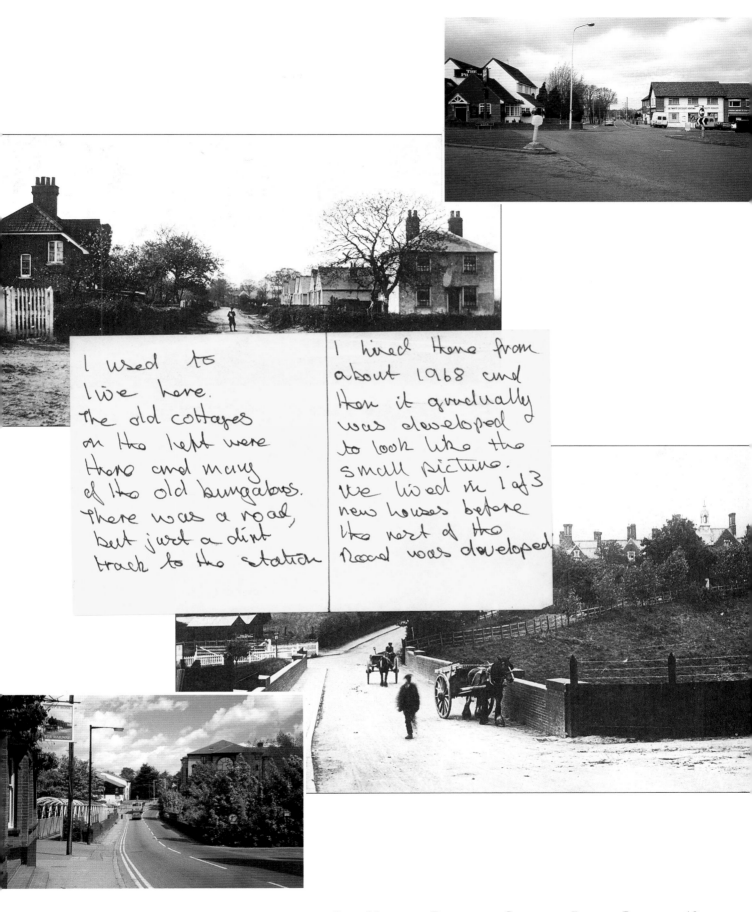

I used to
live here.
The old cottages
on the left were
there and many
of the old bungalows.
There was a road,
but just a dirt
track to the station

I lived there from
about 1968 and
then it gradually
was developed
to look like the
small picture.
We lived in 1 of 3
new houses before
the rest of the
road was developed

This postcard is taken from the entrance to Billericay railway station, facing south towards the High Street. The date is around 1890, with the *Crown Inn* to the east of the road and the *Railway Hotel* to the west. With the exception of the construction of the pedestrian footbridge the scene from this point in 1997 is nearly identical to that of over one hundred years ago.

There has been a *Crown* in Billericay since the 16th century although not on the current site. The existing *Crown* was built in 1889 and stands at the northern end of the High Street by the railway bridge. It opened for business in the months following the arrival of the first passenger steam train service to Billericay on 1 January 1889.

The local taxi service vehicles are lined up in the yard of the *Crown* and those of an earlier era below. The publicity information of the earlier service states, 'Carriages & Traps for Hire. Wedding & Pleasure Parties supplied with up-to-date Carriages & Attendants. Conveyances at Station to meet all Trains.' The vehicle on the left of the main picture is a French Panhard Et Levassor, built in 1908.

This picture is taken from the northern side of the railway bridge towards the High Street. On the southern side of the bridge is the *Crown*, whilst opposite is the *Railway Hotel*, built in 1885.

The scene below shows the riders, horses and hounds of the Essex Union Hounds Meet on 25 March 1911 outside the *Crown*.

BILLERICAY, 690

Towards the High Street, up the small incline from the railway bridge and at the Norsey Road/High Street junction, stood Burstead House, facing south down the High Street. The property was built in the 18th century and demolished in 1958. In the late 1800s/early 1900s it was used as a school and the property became known as the 'Old School House'. It was used as an army headquarters in the Second World War and captured enemy pilots were brought here to be questioned. The above postcard was posted in Billericay on 26 July 1906.

The modern picture (right) was taken at the same location. All the properties in the foreground of the top picture no longer exist.

On travelling east along Norsey Road, away from the High Street, the first road to the south is Crown Road. The properties in the lower part of Crown Road were built during the two world wars by 'Essex Homes Coy. (Billericay) Ltd.'. This company's office was at 'Ye Olde Essex Home', High Street, Billericay which was no.12. The dirt track is now a tarmacked road and the view today is little changed. The view here was taken between the two world wars.

Beyond Crown Road, Norsey Road passes St Andrew's Hospital, which used to be the union workhouse. The above picture was taken c.1905 and is of the Union with the Norsey Road entrance to the left of the picture. The scene is not altered in 1997 with the exception that the entire wall is now covered with foliage and the entrance is blocked.

The picture to the right is of a later date and pictures the houses on the corner of Norsey Road/Highland Grove. The road in the picture is still unmade at the time of the photograph.

Mr. Campbell ran a bus service from Laindon to Billericay and the picture above is of his first two buses.

On the southern side of the Norsey Road/High Street junction, and opposite Burstead House, stood Elizabeth Cottage. In 1704 the building on this site was a Quaker chapel (with burial ground behind) and in 1848, the chapel being dilapidated, the property was sold and became the *Royal Oak* beerhouse. The present Elizabeth Cottage bears the date 1903. (The postcard was posted in Billericay on 10 April 1907.)

Grant McKenzie, a local builder, lived in Elizabeth Cottage from 1912 to 1922. In his *Thoughts on Billericay*, 1989, he describes how the milk was delivered to Elizabeth Cottage: 'Our milk was delivered from Ricketts Diary by Miss Ricketts who carried a large pail with half pint, one pint, etc. cans hanging around the sides of the pail. These she dipped into the pail and the desired amount was emptied into the customer's jug or other receptacle.' The 1895 picture (right) is of workmen repairing the building which was demolished to be replaced in 1903 by Elizabeth Cottage. The sign reads 'Saltwell, Boot & Shoe Maker'.

Ye Old Essex Home, High Street, Billericay.

12 ,14, 16 and 18 High Street are shown on the left of the above picture. No.12 is the building with the oak-framed elevation and is one of the oldest buildings in Billericay. Nos.14, 16 and 18 were formerly one building of 17th-century origin with timber-framed construction. There was once a carriageway through the centre of the building which can be seen in the picture below. This building was originally the *Bull Inn* from *c*.1600 to 1906. The last licensee was Peter Perry, manager to Wells & Perry, brewers of Chelmsford. The card was posted in Billericay on 16 July 1906, written by Peter Perry with the message, 'Have lost the licences, I think it lasts until October'.

On the far right is 26 High Street, which with 28 was the 'Old Bank House' occupied by Sparrow & Co.'s bank. The double doorway was a carriageway to the rear. The bank's business was transferred to Barclays Bank in the late 1900s. Next to it is Hill House, 24 High Street, an 18th-century building which was used by the army in the Second World War.

Sheredays, 22 High Street, is beyond. It was originally built in the 16th century as a small timber-framed house but was later substantially extended, being encased in brickwork in the 18th century. There are various outbuildings, formerly used as coach houses and stables, but now used for a variety of small business including a dress shop, music tuition, fancy dress shop, television repairers and a beauty parlour. In 1996 a large underground room was discovered under one of the outbuildings.

The property was once a boys' academy and one of the illegitimate sons of George IV, George Fit George (born 1808), was a pupil here. Unfortunately he drowned in a nearby pond in 1819. Inside the courtyard entrance pupils 'engraved' their initials with various dates into the red bricks of the north wall of the main building.

The garden, which was more extensive than it is now, is currently a car park. In the past numerous Roman coins have been found at Sheredays from the Roman settlement there.

In 1860 the property was owned by Dr. William Carter and thereafter by his son Frederick, who was also a doctor. When he retired, his partner, Dr. Wells, moved into Sheredays and lived there until his death in 1956. Dr. Wells' cars: a 15 hp Panhard No.F2886 and a 7 hp Panhard No.F2485 are parked outside the garage at 22 High Street. Sheredays is today owned by local solicitor Roger Green.

38 and 40 High Street (immediate right of the picture) are the only two properties to remain today from this section of the High Street. 26 to 36 High Street (beyond 38 and 40 in the picture) were all demolished after the Second World War, as was Burstead House, which can be seen at the north end of the High Street.

38 High Street was built in 1577—the original rear wall had a molded beam inscribed 'THE YEAR OF OUR LORDE 1577 ELIZABETH …'. The construction was of timber with white painted weatherboard. In 1769 this building was the *Magpie & Horseshoes Inn*. It was occupied by the Bassom family from the early 1800s to 1975; the family has been traced back to James Bassom, born *c*.1730. Peter Storey, a local electrician, recalls how he and the then young John Bassom used to enter a tunnel within the building of no.38 and exit in the garden. Some 55 years later attempts are being made to find this tunnel. John Bassom came back to Billericay to point out the entrance but despite extensive digging the tunnel still remains hidden. The house has a deep well and the well head remains today. The property is currently occupied by Roger Green & Company, a firm of solicitors.

40 High Street is the south crosswing of 38 High Street, but built later, though it too was part of the *Magpie & Horseshoes Inn*. It is currently occupied by Raven's the baker.

In the picture below, facing south, 38 & 40 High Street are on the left side of the photograph. Miss Wade's toy and sweet shop was at no.40 in 1938.

The *Chequers* public house, 42-44 High Street, was built in the 16th century and has been an inn since 1765. Built with a central hall with north and south crosswings, it has been altered internally over the years although the low ceilings and beams have been retained. The southern crosswing is currently occupied by a fishmonger's shop. At the rear of the building in Chantry Chase there was a blacksmith's which, like the horse-drawn transport in the picture opposite, is no longer part of Billericay life. In 1468 Billericay was granted a Charter to hold a weekly market and two annual fairs in August and October. The market was held for hundreds of years but eventually declined and ceased at the end of the 19th century. In the early 1920s an attempt was made to revive the Billericay market in the yard at the rear of the *Chequers*, but the attempt failed and it closed within a few months.

Between the *Chequers* and St Mary Magdalen Church a road leads off the High Street and is today known as Chapel Street, though during the last 400 years it has been known by three different names. From 1611 to the 19th century it was known as 'Wellfield Lane', then 'Back Street' but due to the confusion with Back Lane (Western Road), it became known as Chapel Street. (The postcard was posted in Billericay on 22 August 1903.)

On the corner stands the war memorial. A stone cross, to the memory of the Billericay men who died in the First World War, was erected in 1921 and a second memorial was erected in 1957 (at the rear) in memory of those who lost their lives in the Second World War. The area was originally enclosed by iron railings but these were taken down and used for the war effort in the Second World War.

The picture below is of the dedication of the war memorial.

1 Chapel Street is the south crosswing of the original *Chequers* building and was used as a baker's from 1862. H.J. Swayne (top) baked at the Chapel Street Bakery until after the First World War and the property continued to be used as a bakery until the early 1930s. In 1936 Mr. Goodspeed purchased the building and commenced trading as a fishmonger and 'GoodsPeeds' is still operated today by his descendants.

Next to 13 Chapel Street, set back from the road, was Billericay fire station. It had a large sliding door and housed the fire engine until 1939. Before fire brigades were controlled by the local parish councils, most fire brigades were established by the insurance companies who insured properties against fire. If you were insured, then the fire brigades would attend a fire; to prove you were insured an insurance plaque would be affixed to your building. A 'Royal' plaque is affixed to Three Horseshoes House whilst another is affixed to Sheredays, 22 High Street.

The four weavers' cottages which originally occupied the site of the cinema in Chapel Street were demolished *c.*1900. The land was used for allotments until the construction of the Ritz by the Billericay Cinema Company. The Ritz opened on Easter Monday in 1938 as a single-storey auditorium with capacity for 650 people. Its use as a cinema ceased in 1971 and thereafter the building was used as a bingo hall. Its current use as a snooker hall commenced in 1992. Externally there has been little alteration since the building was constructed.

Further south along Chapel Street the Tannery Cottages (the tops of which were plastered and the bottom halves weatherboarded) stood opposite the old burial ground. The cottages were demolished in 1939 and in their place were erected two wooden huts used for military purposes during the Second World War. The earliest documentary reference to the old burial ground was on 2 July 1692. In the grounds there is a vault in which were placed three large stone coffins. Harry Richman, in his book *Billericay and its High Street*, concludes 'that as interment of the entire body was contemporaneous with cremation amongst the Romans renders it not altogether unreasonable to suppose them to belong to that period'. The wall and the burial ground behind remain undisturbed.

All the pictures on this page look north, back up Chapel Street towards the High Street. On the right-hand side of the top picture is the Congregational Church (now the United Reformed Church) which was built in 1838. Opposite is Rose Hall, which was built in 1850 as a school. In the Second World War this was used as a mess room for the soldiers who were billeted in the town. The row of cottages in the middle picture of *c*.1909 were in existence in 1849 and remain today, although the properties to the north no longer stand.

St Mary Magdalen Church stands in the middle of the High Street. The drawing above epitomises life in 1830.

Around 1342 a chapel and chantry were founded in Billericay. The west tower of St Mary Magdalen is of 15th-century origin and would have been built on the site of an existing church. The tower is the oldest part of the church and was restored in 1880. The rest of the building is of brick of 1780 when the then existing chapel was rebuilt. The clock commemorates Queen Victoria's Diamond Jubilee, whilst the font is 18th-century and parish registers date from 1844.

From the buildings that comprised 46 to 60 High Street, only nos.46 and 48 remain in 1997. Nos.50 to 60 have all been demolished and replaced since the Second World War.

Next to St Mary Madgalen is no.46, Church House, and no.48, both of early 18th-century construction and, in fact, originally one building. Church House is today in a state of dilapidation (although renovation works have commenced in October 1997) whilst no.48 is occupied by 'Presence', a small gift shop with a coffee lounge above. The window cleaners' ladders are leaning against no. 50 in the picture postcard above (posted in Billericay on 15 October 1908).

Nos.52 to 56 were the site of the *George*, one of the original Billericay inns, being in existence in 1563 and closing between the years 1738 and 1765.

Mr. Howard had a newsagent's shop at no.60 before moving to larger premises at nos.54/56. In the left postcard (posted in Billericay on 10 June 1919) Mr. Howard stands at the entrance to his shop at no.60, whilst in the view below the awning of his shop at 54/56 can be seen.

62 and 64 High Street, occupied by Mr. Larritt, are to the left of the above left picture, with 66 High Street just beyond. Of 62 to 84 High Street (shown below) only nos.72 and 74 remain in 1997, the remainder having been demolished and replaced. No.72 is one of the oldest buildings in Billericay, being built in the 16th century. It is timber-framed with a plastered exterior. Internally the oak beams are exposed and the building is currently occupied by 'Aquilla', an optician's. No.74 is of 18th-century origin and is occupied by the Cater Museum with two shops on the ground floor. The museum, which was officially opened on 7 May 1960, is a must for anyone who has an interest in Billericay history.

David Savill occupied various buildings in Billericay whilst carrying on his second-hand furniture business. He had 17 children and died in 1914 aged sixty. The postcard above right shows Mr. Savill standing outside his antique shop at 66 High Street with his wife and some of his children. The card was posted in Billericay by Mr. Savill on 28 September 1907; the message reads: ' Dear Sir, Re purchase of this morning the hammer was packed up with Mr Thorne's tools. If you write him undoubtedly he will send it on to you'. Today 66 High Street is Boot's the chemist.

The two gentlemen in the main picture below are standing outside 84 High Street which was Cottis the bakers (shown left in this 1921 picture). No.84 was redeveloped in 1985, the only part of the building not being demolished being the front wall and the roof facing the road.

In the picture below, Mr. Layland stands outside 72 High Street in front of his surveying and valuation business.

With the exception of no.86 (which was demolished and replaced by a supermarket), 86 to 94 High Street remain today as they were in the early 1900s. This entire section was the site of the original *Crown Inn* (with its brewery on the land to the rear) from 1611 to 1859. Nos.88 to 90 were constructed in Edwardian style in the early 1900s. No.92 was a butcher's shop in 1867 and, after being rebuilt, has been used for that trade for the last 77 years. In 1962 the last Billericay slaughter house on this site closed.

High Street, Billericay.

No.94 (far right, above) was built in 1830 as a market house with grammar school and assembly room. In 1862 part of the ground floor was used as a police station (with the cells at the rear) and on the first floor was the court room. 'ESSEX CONSTABULARY' can be seen across the front of the building's fascia in the picture although these words have now been removed from the building itself.

No.94 remained a police station until 1939 and after the war became the council chamber for the Billericay Urban District Council. In 1997 it is in a state of dilapidation although essential repairs have been carried out over the last two years. The top picture of the policeman in the vehicle was taken at the rear of the police station.

96 to 104 High Street have all survived and can still be seen in 1997. The postcard right was posted in Billericay in August 1906 and at that time no.96 did not exist, but when built it adjoined the old police station. 98 High Street was built *c.*1744 and was the *Maiden Head Inn* until 1810. In the First World War it was the headquarters of the Home Guard. Terry Gregson and P.J. Murray, insurance consultants, are now its occupants. Foxcroft, 100 High Street, is also an 18th-century house. In 1930 it became a children's home and in 1979 offices, being currently occupied by solicitors Roger Green & Company. No.102 is an Edwardian property which stands on the site of a 16th/17th-century property which originally formed part of the building next door.

To the far right of the above picture is 104 High Street, a 16th-century property which became the post office in the late 1800s and was the main post office for the area until 1938, since when it has been a jeweller's and watchmaker's. It was in this building on 3 July 1996 that the owner Julian Shone was shot and murdered during a jewellery raid whilst going about his daily business. His killers were caught and are now in prison. A memorial plaque and clock have been erected to his memory on the north wall of the building.

The fire-fighting ability of the local fire brigade is demonstrated outside 98 and 100 High Street, keenly watched by the crowd (left).

The modern scene is little changed from that of over 100 years ago (below).

108 to 112 High Street are the first three properties from the left in the above and right pictures.

108 High Street is timber-framed and was built in the 17th century with a central block and north and south crosswings. There is a ground-level entrance through the north crosswing to the land at the rear. It was in this building in 1884 that the first Roman Catholic mass was said since the Reformation. From 1934 to 1955 this property was occupied by the Billericay Urban District Council.

110 High Street was a late 16th-century property which was demolished in 1960. 112 High Street was an early 18th-century double-fronted red-brick building. Both properties have been replaced by modern shops. The top picture, c.1905, features the road cleaner going about his daily task.

114, 116 and 118 High Street are the first three properties from the left in both pictures. St Edith's can be seen on the right-hand side in the picture below. (This postcard was posted in Barking on 11 January 1906.) 114 High Street was an 18th-century house and at this time was being used as a newsagent's and tobacconist's. It was in this building that the first Billericay telephone exchange was established, at which time Billericay had 24 numbers and the railway station was number 1. 116 High Street was originally known as Dryden House and, like both its neighbours, was of 18th-century origin. 118 High Street was a tall red-brick house with a parapet and the home of the Cheyne Library until it was destroyed by fire in 1956. The fire, which claimed the life of the owner Mrs. Melville, also damaged the adjoining property no.116. Both properties remained derelict until they were demolished in 1958 to be replaced by the large building which, until they went into liquidation, was occupied by Rumbelows. It is rumoured that 118 High Street was haunted by the ghost of a miser (who hanged himself in the cellar after his savings were stolen) and a young girl (who was seen on the staircase).

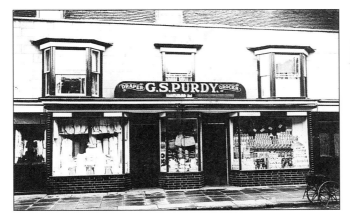

128 High Street was occupied by G.S. Purdy, draper and grocer from 1912 to 1954.

The view of the postcard above is of 120 to 128 High Street looking north, with 128 High Street to the right of the picture. The card was posted in Billericay on 20 September 1907. 128 High Street was built in *c.*1775, refronted in 1918 and demolished in 1955. In the picture it is being used for a linen and woollen draper. From the number of children in the picture it can only be assumed that this was a weekday and the children were returning to their homes after leaving the school in Laindon Road. At the time of the photograph, 120 High Street did not exist, the land being a piece of garden ground. In 1922 a building was constructed on this land and in due course it became the home of the local district nurse. In 1986 the 1922 building was demolished and the present shop was constructed. 122 to 126 High Street was of 17th-century origin and consisted of one building with a central gable and projecting wings. From *c.*1860 to 1890 it was the *Crown* beerhouse. The whole building was demolished in 1963 to make way for its modern replacement.

With the exception of the *White Hart Inn* (138 High Street) nos.130 to 136 have all been demolished and replaced. In 130 High Street the town crier used to live, while 132 and 134 High Street were part of the same 16th-century property. The entrance to the Walk, a modern shopping and office development, is between nos.128 and 130. No.136 (the right-hand property) was a 17th-century timber-framed building which was replaced by the post office building in 1938 and the telephone exchange (at the rear) was opened in 1952. This was the second property in the High Street to have an alleged ghost—'a young woman in white'.

The original *White Hart* was on the site of 69 High Street at the beginning of the 17th century, transferring to the current site in about 1765 to 1772. The *White Hart* was originally in 1724 the *Star Inn*; therefore there has been an inn or public house on this site for at least 273 years. The sign on the front wall used to declare the brewery as 'Russell's Gravesend Brewery'. The view in the picture on the right is looking southwards with the *White Hart Inn* on the left and Laindon Road in the distance.

No.146, Bleak House is to the far right of the top picture; 140 to 144 High Street can be seen beyond. 140 and 142 High Street are two 18th-century properties which are today a furniture store; no.144 was a 17th-century building, weather-boarded on the front, but with brick to the rear. The property was badly shaken by a blast in the Second World War and it had to be demolished thereafter. Bleak House was an 18th-century brick building which was demolished some 20 years ago and rebuilt in identical form by the Hamber Brothers, a local building firm. The children appear to be standing in a circle playing a game in the middle of the High Street; this would be an impossibility in 1997.

Next to Bleak House is the last property on the eastern side of the High Street: no.148. The building was used by hay and corn merchants and was sold to Cramphorns in 1923. At that time the shop front of the building had not yet been developed. Opposite, on the west side of the road, is the site where the police station was built in 1938. Subsequently the whole property was replaced with the modern shop and offices which exist in 1997.

Sun Inn and London Road, Billericay.

At the end of the High Street is Sun Street which at its end forms a junction with Chapel Street (to the north) and Southend Road (to the south). On the opposite side to 148 High Street, on the Sun Street/Laindon Road corner, stands the *Rising Sun Hotel*. There was a building on this site in 1593 and the current building is 18th century; the hotel opened for business in 1810. It soon became a busy coaching inn and in 1823 coaches left from it every day for London and Southend

Beyond the *Rising Sun* (below) is a weather-boarded cottage where a Mr. Totman lived. He was a cattle drover who took animals to and from the Chelmsford and Romford markets before the days of cattle lorries.

A farmhouse known as Quilters (taking its name from its occupiers) stood on the other side of the *Rising Sun*. This was demolished *c*.1930 after lying derelict for several years and is on the far right of the above picture.

From behind the *Rising Sun*, south down the Laindon Road to the Catholic Church was the Weir Pond. It was 15 feet in width but not of any depth. In winter, when the ice was hard enough, it was used for skating. After the Second World War it was drained and filled in and, as can be seen from the picture on the above left, the scene is now totally different. (The postcard above right was posted in Billericay on 7 September 1904.)

This picture of the Weir Pond, looks north towards the High Street with the *Rising Sun Hotel* in the distance on the right-hand side of the Laindon Road. Also on the right can be seen the iron tower of the Southern Waterworks Company, which was fed from water being pumped from the well at Slicers Gate, Great Burstead, and supplied the town. The iron tower was demolished and replace by a concrete tower which remains today. The 1997 photograph left shows how the scene has altered, though the water tower is still visible behind the buildings.

When Billericay became a parish in 1910, the Ursuline sisters from Brentwood leased 129 High Street, later known as St Edith's. A chapel was created and some thirty people attended the first mass there on 10 July 1910. The sisters from Brentwood left in 1913 and, immediately after their departure, building of the Church of the Most Holy Redeemer commenced in 1913. The first part of the church was opened on 20 July 1919 but the building was not completed until 1926.

The left picture shows how the church was in 1926. The three statues, which were in the niches above the main door, and the original war memorial crucifix are no longed there. The porch was added in 1981 and, although there was provision for two bells in the belfry, there has only ever been one. Opposite on the other side of the road was the Great Burstead Board Schools.

The picture above is of a group of first communicants outside the church.

On the east side of the Laindon Road was the school. It was the only school serving the town and all the children in Billericay had to come here. A stone in the centre of the front states 'Great Burstead Board Schools 1878', although later it was known as the Council School and later still as Quilters. In 1997 it is partly used as a restaurant and public house whilst the remainder is The Fold, Billericay's Art Centre. The surrounding fields have been developed and the only view today is a restricted one from the road.

The girls of the Council School gather for a school photograph behind the gardening lesson in 1912 (above).

A May-Day Procession within the school grounds in 1931 (right).

The Billericay carnival fancy dress competition in 1934 was held in the field behind the school (left).

The Billericay carnival competition of 1931 (below).

Along Laindon Road signs for two Scout groups announce their presence in 1997. Unfortunately the postcard shown here is undated and very faded.

Built in 1930, the Archer Memorial Church Hall was not only used for church purposes but also for public meetings, ballet shows and sports events. The land was left to the church by Miss Archer of Little Burstead and it was originally intended to build a church. In the 1990s that objective was finally achieved with the demolition of Archer Hall and the building of Emmanuel.

Two of the events which were hosted by the Archer Hall: *above*—one of the many Billericay Horticultural Shows; *below*—a photograph of the famous Billericay general election count in 1959 when the result was declared only 57 minutes after the closing of the voting booths. It was a major achievement, with fast cars bringing the ballot boxes to the Archer Hall from as far as South Weald and Bowers Gifford, hundreds of volunteers from everywhere assisting with the count, and BBC cameras broadcasting the event live. The voting booths closed at 9 o'clock and the result was declared at 9.57 pm after 100,000 votes had been counted. The record lasted until 1997 when Sunderland declared at 9.47 pm, albeit with only 50,000 votes.

Weir Cottages are on the left-hand side of Laindon Road looking towards the High Street in this early 1900s view. In 1997 only two of the cottages remain (below) and these are empty and in a state of dilapidation, although renovation work has now commenced.

Weir Cottages can be clearly seen in the distance and Laindon Road is only a dirt track with the gas lamp giving limited illumination in this early 1900s picture.

Mrs. Troute is in the doorway of her cottage (left), which was opposite the Church of the Most Holy Redeemer on the Laindon Road.

This is the junction of Brentwood Road and London Road with Western Road and Tye Common Road. The signpost below indicates Little Burstead 2, Ingrave 4, Billericay Stn and Stock 3. The sole delivery van stands outside 'Hart's Corner' in the picture below whilst customers' cars are parked outside (left). This building was damaged by a bomb in the Second World War, demolished and replaced by a garage.

The police station was erected on this corner site of High Street and London Road in 1938. Within the building were two courts but these are no longer operational. Prior to the construction of the station, this site was a meadow used for grazing.

Of 151 to 147 High Street, number 151 High Street is to the far left of the right picture, dating from *c.*1906. This was a large two-storey building constructed in the 18th century and used as a grocer's and draper's from 1848 to 1948. To the north were three cottages which were all demolished prior to the Second World War and replaced by a modern brick house. Eventually this and 151 High Street were demolished to be replaced by Audit House and KFC house, which are modern office buildings. The modern picture shows the changing scenery; Burghstead Lodge is hidden by foliage behind the red brick wall.

The two riders and dogs of the Essex Hounds have passed the *Three Horse Shoes* (137 and 139 High Street) and are coming level with the Old Shambles (133 and 135 High Street). In the yard at the rear of this 18th-century property was a very deep well with a large iron pump which is still in existence. The property was once used as a butcher's and the building beyond, next to the *Three Horse Shoes*, was used for the storage of the butcher's horse and cart and the animals awaiting slaughter. On the cessation of the business the building became the *Old Shambles Hotel* and thereafter offices. The southern end of the *Three Horse Shoes* is of 17th-century origin and an inn was on this site from 1765 to 1912 (the old inn sign bracket still projects from the building). The northern section of the building is younger and the northern wall has a stone with the date 'A.D.1885' carved on it.

The Old Shambles is to the left of the picture below with the view looking north.

St Edith's, situated at the southern end of the High Street, was constructed in two sections. The northern end of the building was built *c.*1840 and the southern end, in Gothic style, in 1863. The splendid iron railings at the front of the building were removed in the Second World War to be used in the manufacture of armaments. The building has been used as a school, a holiday home for East End girls, a private residence and for public worship. In 1940 it was requisitioned for use as an army rest centre and later, until 1958, as a nurses' home for nurses working at St Andrew's. Demolished in 1961, its replacement is a modern office block (shown left), built in 1963.

115 and 117 High Street were originally one 16th-century building. From 1860 until 1894, 117 High Street was a boys' academy and from 1910 to 1940 was the *Burstead House Temperance Hotel*, although at some time it was called *The Temperance Hotel*. As in days past the hotel offered various services including stables, loose boxes and the hiring of horses and pony traps. In the Second World War the building was used as the local food office. 115 High Street was mainly used as a private residence although in 1873 there was a girls' academy here. Both properties were demolished after the war and a garage was erected, including petrol pumps and workshops. The garage became Hensman's but that itself was demolished in the 1960s to make way for the existing supermarket, shops and offices. (The postcard was posted in Billericay on 6 July 1914.)

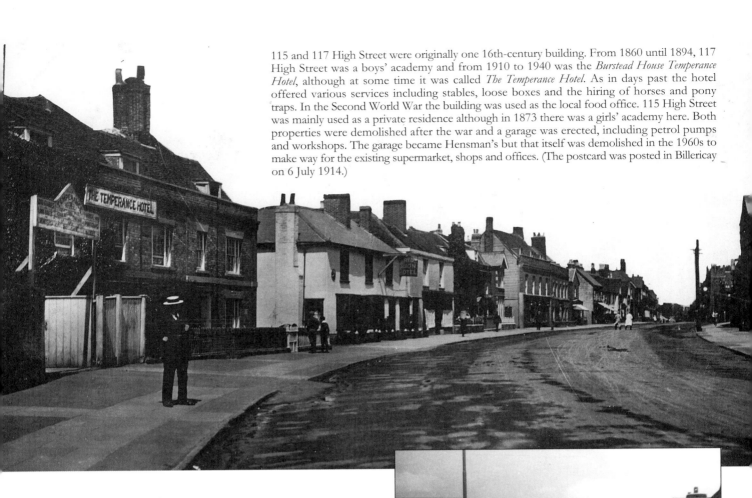

In the picture right, 121, 123 and 125 High Street are the three red-brick cottages on the left of the picture. The only aspect of note was a carving on the chimney stack of 121 which had the shape of a crowned head facing the High Street. The scene in 1997 shows the new buildings that now stand on the site of nos.121 to 115.

Alongside 115 High Street and prior to reaching the *Red Lion* is Lion Lane, which runs from the High Street to Western Road. Lion Lane is completely developed in 1997 although it has retained its charm. The top postcard was posted in Billericay on 7 August 1935, the wagon being loaded with trees. The bottom left postcard was posted on 24 December 1921 and shows a woman looking over the field gate to fields which no longer exist.

The *Red Lion* is of 15th-century origin and is one of the oldest buildings in Billericay. There has been an inn on this site from 1593 until the present, although until 1804 the inn incorporated the adjoining property at 111 High Street. With the decline of the coaching trade 111 High Street became a private residence. In the picture below the Essex Hunt gathers outside the *Red Lion* and its adjoining premises, Nix the chemist. The building of no.111 remains today and a chemist business has been carried on here since 1812.

Of 99 to 109 High Street only 99 and 103 have not been demolished and replaced. No.103 has been extensively modernised whilst 99 High Street remains the same with the exception of a new shop front. The above picture was taken at the turn of the century (posted in Billericay on 21 March 1907). Notice the railings outside nos.109, 107 and 101. The children on the left are standing outside 109 High Street which is the ivy-covered building; today this is Midland Bank. The horse and carriage are outside no.103 (video store and building society) whilst in the middle of the picture the boy with his smaller brother in the hand cart is outside 101 High Street (now Woolworth's).

A view of the High Street in the very early 1900s, facing south, is shown left. The property on the right of the picture was Houghton's, a draper's and grocer's, 103 High Street. In the middle of the picture is a wagon delivering supplies to the *Red Lion Hotel*, whilst St Edith's and the adjoining cottages can be clearly seen. On the opposite side of the road numbers 98, 100 and 102 are visible.

91 High Street is the white building with the two gables in the picture above. The building is of mid-16th-century timber frame and plaster and it was in this building that the Billericay Independent Protestant Dissenters met in 1672. A plaque is attached to the front of the building commemorating this event. To the north is 89 High Street which was constructed in 1890 and is now Lloyds Bank. In 1900 iron railings and hedges were in front of 91-95 High Street.

97 High Street is to the far left of the bottom left picture. In this 1900 photograph the property was being used as draper's, outfitter's, milliner's and a haircutting and shaving salon. In 1949 it became Billericay's first library under the Essex County Council. The building was demolished in the 1980s and is now the Abbey National. Beyond is 93 and 95 High Street, a late 16th-century/early 17th-century timber-framed building which is in existence in 1997. In 1765 this property was the *Hare & Hounds Inn*.

C.J. Taylor was a corn merchant who lived at 89 High Street. He is pictured below by the side of his Foden Steam Wagon fully loaded with corn.

Out of 73 to 87 High Street, nos.73 to 79 remain today. 81 to 87 High Street (on the left, bottom picture) were brick-fronted 17th-century houses of oak construction. They were demolished in 1972 and replaced by shops and offices. The Shelly family currently occupy 75 to 79 High Street which are some of the oldest buildings in Billericay. They are of oak-frame construction and were built in the early 1500s. There is an opening between 77 and 79 giving access to the rear and to Mr. Shelly's garage. This propery was the *White Lyon Inn* from 1685 to 1809. 73 High Street (right, top picture) is the reading rooms built in 1886. At the time of construction they were at the centre of Billericay activity and, although their use has declined, they are still used today by many organisations.

69 High Street was a private residence until 1922 when it was purchased by Barclay's Bank. The original building was mostly 18th-century and can been seen to the left of the picture (right). This building was demolished in 1956 when the current one was erected. On this site from 1638 to 1772 was the *White Hart Inn*.

65 to 67 High Street (currently Kingston's, the butcher's) was constructed as one house in the 17th century. A double-fronted shop was installed in the 1920s with the current front built in 1959/60. This is the shop in the picture below with 'C.F. Podd' on its facade. Further north (second from left) is 63 High Street which, despite its 18th/19th-century facade, is a 16th/17th-century building.

In 1342 a Chancery Chapel, with sufficient lands to support a priest, was founded in Billericay. 57 to 61 High Street are believed to have been the site of the priest's house. The existing buildings were originally one house, built in *c.*1510 of timber-frame construction, consisting of a central hall with gabled north and south crosswings. There are numerous exposed beams in the properties.

Its main link with the past is that legend states (although there is no documentary proof) that Christopher Martin, the Governor of the *Mayflower* (the ship that sailed the Pilgrim Fathers to America) lived here. There is evidence that he owned property in the High Street but it is doubtful that it was on this side of the street. Five inhabitants of Billericay left to join the *Mayflower* at Grays or Leigh. Christopher Martin travelled across the Atlantic with his wife, a servant, a relative named Solomon Prower and a John Browne from Outwood Common. Unfortunately, they all died in the first winter after arrival due to illness. It has been suggested that the Essex contingent for the *Mayflower* gathered in Billericay prior to joining the ship. On 23 May 1655 the new town of Billerica was established by the Massachusetts Legislature following a petition by Billericay emigrants.

Christopher Martin's House, Billericay

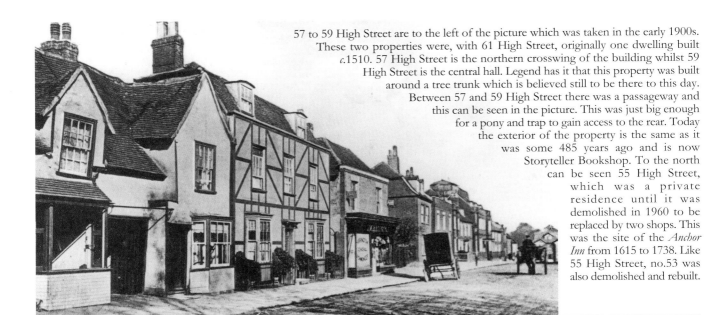

57 to 59 High Street are to the left of the picture which was taken in the early 1900s. These two properties were, with 61 High Street, originally one dwelling built *c.*1510. 57 High Street is the northern crosswing of the building whilst 59 High Street is the central hall. Legend has it that this property was built around a tree trunk which is believed still to be there to this day. Between 57 and 59 High Street there was a passageway and this can be seen in the picture. This was just big enough for a pony and trap to gain access to the rear. Today the exterior of the property is the same as it was some 485 years ago and is now Storyteller Bookshop. To the north can be seen 55 High Street, which was a private residence until it was demolished in 1960 to be replaced by two shops. This was the site of the *Anchor Inn* from 1615 to 1738. Like 55 High Street, no.53 was also demolished and rebuilt.

Of 39 to 51 High Street only no.39 has been completely demolished. No.53 is the property to the left of the bottom picture with the horse and cart standing outside. Next, to the north, was the front garden of Crescent House. The railings and front wall were removed in 1952 and replaced by two shops with a central archway for access to Crescent House. 49 High Street is an 18th-century property and now has a shop front. Legend says that this was the site of the *Blue Boar Tavern* but there is no documentary proof of this. 45 and 47 High Street are both late 17th-century and remain today, albeit with shop fronts. 43 High Street was demolished with the exception of the front elevation which was retained and the new property built behind. 41 High Street remains today and is the National Westminster Bank. 39 High Street is the building with the look-out tower on the roof. Major Spitty lived here and he was responsible for the construction of Lake Meadows. The building was requisitioned by the army in the Second World War and a gun was placed in the lookout. The property was of 16th-century origin and was demolished in 1958 to make way for the Co-operative Society supermarket.

The bay shop window to the right of the picture is 23 High Street, with 25 and 27 High Street being part of the same set of cottages. The double-fronted house beyond is 33 High Street which is an 18th-century timber-framed building with brickwork superimposed over the woodwork. Despite the difference in appearance today it is in fact the same structure. This property has for many years been used by Mr. Farrer the undertaker.

The middle picture is of workmen replacing defective timbers and creating a new front wall at 33 High Street.

In the bottom picture Dr. Wells, who used to live at 22 High Street, is driving his 15 hp Panhard, registration number F2886. Behind the car can be seen, to the left of the picture, 35 and 37 High Street with numbers 23 to 33 to the right. 35 and 37 High Street were both demolished in 1957 and replaced.

In 1997 there is no resemblance to the past at the end of the High Street. All the properties in the 1905 picture above no longer exist. Both the pictures on this page were taken from the same position. 23-27 High Street were 17th/18th-century timber-framed properties and, with nos.29 and 31, were demolished in 1962 to be replaced by shops with flats above. 27 High Street is now a travel agent's, no.25 a sports shop and no.23 a hairdressing salon. 21 High Street was demolished and in 1911 a new shop was built which for many years was used by the Co-operative Society.

Despite being some 300 years old in the 1960s, 17 and 19 High Street were demolished to improve the traffic flow at the High Street/Western Road corner. If you look carefully at the photograph you can observe the horse and wagon exiting from Western Road. (The postcard above was posted in Billericay on 6 August 1908.)

Unfortunately there is no date for the Christmas photograph of the manager and his staff of the Billericay Branch of the Brentwood & District Provident Co-Operative Society, Limited at 21 High Street. Grocery provisions, a hamper and bottles of wine are for sale in the left-hand window with clothes and Christmas crackers in the right. The building is now divided into two shops, a basement restaurant and a first-floor fitness studio. The Chelmsford Co-operative Society now has a super-market at 39 High Street.

This picture is taken from the Norsey Road/High Street junction looking south. The building to the right of the picture is 21 High Street which used to be the Co-operative shop. Observe in the 1997 picture the scar on the side of this building from the demolition of 19 High Street when the Western Road junction was improved.

Norsey View, a three-storey, red-brick building, stood at the junction of Western Road and the High Street. In its life it had been used as a private residence, place of worship, vicarage, doctor's surgery and for the billeting of soldiers. Demolished in 1947, it was replaced by shops and flats.

At the northern end of the High Street, opposite Norsey Road, is Western Road. In 1595 it was known as Newe Street, in the 1700s as Back Lane and from the early 1900s as Western Road. The northern side of the junction has been completely demolished and replaced by modern shops and flats but the southern side remains. The three pictures on this page are taken looking towards the High Street and all from nearly the same position. The older pictures were taken 1910 to 1915. You can observe the squad of soldiers (left) lined up for inspection, with Burstead House in the background.

Tanfield Drive is the first road on the right going west along Western Road from its junction with the High Street. It is one of the oldest roads in Billericay, taking it name from the tannery which once existed there. The property on the far right of the picture above had a flat roof with an unusual parapet wall above the roof which gave the appearance of a castle. The castle has been demolished and replaced by flats but the houses in the foreground remain today.

All three pictures below are of Western Road. The top inset was taken in 1914; the main postcard was written by someone staying at Burstead House and posted in Billericay in 1916. The horse and trap is alongside an early version of a motor bike and sidecar. The lady in the picture is holding a parrot on her arm. (The bottom inset postcard was posted in Billericay on 13 May 1929.)

Station Road

Tye Common Road

New Lodge

Heading towards Little Burstead down Western Road, Station Road is passed on the right-hand side. Why this road is called Station Road is quite a mystery because it is nowhere near any station. At the end of Western Road there is a crossroads with Brentwood Road, London Road and Tye Common Road. Crossing over the junction, Tye Common Road meanders towards Little Burstead. The road passes the site where the New Lodge Sanatorium used to stand at the corner of Blunts Wall Road prior to it being demolished following a fire. The site has been redeveloped with private housing abutting the road. (The middle postcard was posted in Billericay on 1 October 1910; the bottom postcard on 14 July 1913.)

Along Tye Common Road, but prior to reaching the Green at Little Burstead, Stockwell Hall is on the left-hand side. It has an 18th-century front with 16th/17th-century older parts behind. The main rooms behind the front have Jacobean panelling and fireplaces; the hall has a moat to the rear and a well. At the southern end of the building there is a large clock in the gable, the figures on the clock being formed from blackened human bones which are said to date from the time of the Civil War. (The postcard of the bridge over the moat was posted in Herongate on 17 August 1926 and the card of the Old Oak in Billericay on 22 March 1926.)

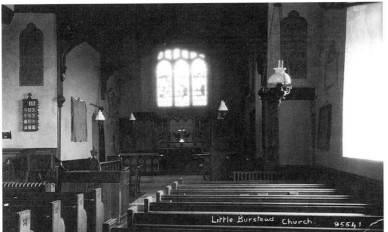

Before turning left into Laindon Common Road at the Green, bear right into Rectory Road where at the bend in the road the Church of St Mary the Virgin is on the right. It is a small 13th-century church built of puddingstone and ragstone with a turret and two bells of 15th-century origin (although there are later 14th- and 15th-century additions). The registers date from 1681. For naval historians, in the chancel lies Sir George Walton who, when serving under Admiral Rodney, captured a squadron of Spanish ships. Opposite the entrance to the church is a footpath which links directly with Great Burstead.

From the Green, bear left down Laindon Common Road and Little Burstead School is on the right. The views in these pictures are looking back down Laindon Common Road with Little Burstead School in the distance. The foundation stone of the school reads 'Little Burstead School 1891'.

LITTLE BURSTEAD. 694.

At the junction of Clockhouse Road, Laindon Common Road and Rectory Road is the Green at Little Burstead. The property that can be seen in the left picture is Hope House, an 18th-century building. After the Second World War the property was used as a boys' preparatory school and later it was converted into four houses. The war memorial is dedicated to the memory of eight men who died in the First World War and also eight men who died in the Second World War.

Past the school, the village pond is on the right-hand side and, with the exception of the growth of foliage and the track now made up, the scene has not substantially altered. Beyond the pond was Little Burstead post office, now demolished and replaced by modern housing. (The right-hand postcard was posted in Billericay on 26 August 1913.)

The weather-boarded timber-framed properties (below) are on the left-hand side of the road after passing the pond and the post office and are shown here in 1936. The *Wheatsheaf* public house was a Charringtons Brewery House before conversion into a private dwelling.

LITTLE BURSTEAD. 693.

Fred Spalding. Photo Chelmsford. Copyright.

On the left-hand side of Laindon Common Road was The Forge, Little Burstead. This picture (right) was taken in 1912 and is of James Carpenter and, to his right, his son, Thomas. The family were in charge of the forge for some four generations. The forge was demolished some years ago and replaced by a modern house.

Towards Laindon Common, along Laindon Common Road, there are various properties scattered on both sides of the roadway. All remain today but the appearance of many of them has substantially altered.

The *Duke's Head Inn* on Laindon Common, Little Burstead is shown above. Its beers and ales were supplied by Baddow Brewery of Chelmsford.

The picture below left is of the small bridge crossing the River Crouch on the Laindon Common Road with the sign and entrance to the *Duke's Head* on the right-hand side. The modern picture is of the same view.

The picture below is a side view of the *Duke's Head* on Laindon Common, looking towards Little Burstead. The *Duke's Head* was in existence as a public house in 1826 and has since been extended.

   The bottom picture is taken from the village side of the public house's entrance/exit way. The properties in the picture are now hidden by foliage when viewed from the same position today, but although the exterior colour has been changed to white the same cottages still exist, and are known as Brook Cottages.

Once Laindon Common has been crossed, the main Billericay to Basildon road is met, which for this section, is Noak Hill Road. In the above picture the property which can be seen on the left is Stockwell House, now completely hidden by trees.

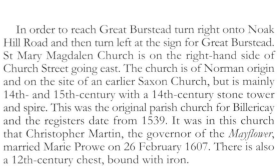

GREAT S

In order to reach Great Burstead turn right onto Noak Hill Road and then turn left at the sign for Great Burstead. St Mary Magdalen Church is on the right-hand side of Church Street going east. The church is of Norman origin and on the site of an earlier Saxon Church, but is mainly 14th- and 15th-century with a 14th-century stone tower and spire. This was the original parish church for Billericay and the registers date from 1539. It was in this church that Christopher Martin, the governor of the *Mayflower*, married Marie Prowe on 26 February 1607. There is also a 12th-century chest, bound with iron.

Old Oak Chest (12 Century) Gt. Burstead.

Great Burstead Church Interior

On the north side of Church Street, prior to reaching the church, was Hillcrest Farm. In the picture on the previous page the pony and trap are level with the farm. To the west of the church were two cottages and a butcher's shop. By the 1980s the two cottages had become one and the shop was the village stores. The shop has now completely disappeared and the three cottages comprise one residence. The picture above with the cottages, shop and church in the background dates from the early 1900s.

To the west of the church was Well Farm (top). Left is a 1900 picture of Bottle Cottages.

To the east of St Mary Magdalen, Church Street continues and becomes Mill Road. At the bend in the road the first turning on the left is Kennel Lane.

On the night of 23/24 September 1916 L-32 Zeppelin, commanded by Oberleutnant zur See Werner Peterson was shot down by Flight-Lieutenant Souray and crashed into the fields off Jackson's Lane. The top picture is of the wrecked Zeppelin being guarded by soldiers with the crowds in the fields beyond.

The bottom picture is of the body of Commander Peterson being carried by soldiers away from the wreck. The bodies of all the Zeppelin crew were buried in Great Burstead Church graveyard.

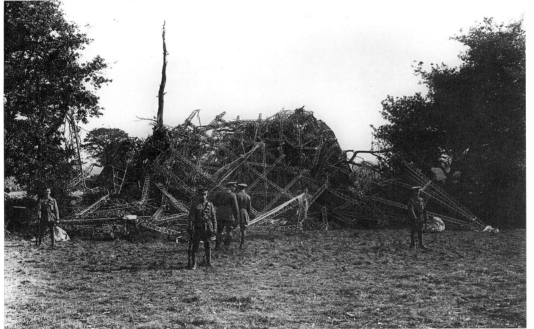

The pilots who shot down these craft became heroes, as seen by the postcard 'THEY FEAR NO FOE'. The government censor had to sanction and approve any publication in respect of these incidents.

The remains of the crew of the Zeppelin were buried on the west side of Great Burstead Church graveyard. The left marker stated 'Commander V Peterson. German Airman. Died 23/Sept/16'; the right stated '21 Unknown German Airmen. 23/Sep/16.' The bodies were exhumed from Great Burstead churchyard in the 1960s and removed to the German War Graves Cemetery at Cannock, Staffordshire, though evidence of the German graves can still be seen today.

A ceremony which was held at the graveside of the German airmen on 28 October 1936. Note the Nazi salute by the German standing on the graves and the Nazi flag. It was an international affair where flags of various countries were presented.

THE ZEPPELIN HEROES.

FLIGHT-LIEUTENANT SOURAY,
who brought down Zeppelin in
Essex on 23rd September, 1916.

FLIGHT-LIEUTENANT ROBINSON, V.C.,
who brought down Zeppelin at
Cuffley on 2nd September, 1916.

THEY FEAR NO FOE.

The 1909 picture and the modern photograph are taken from approximately the same position, although nearly 90 years separate the two scenes. The view is northwards up Kennel Lane, with Church Street behind and Trinity Road to the right. The setting was entirely rural with open fields, but the area has now been substantially developed. If you look carefully at the thatched roof, half way up on the right-hand side a building can be seen. This is Acors, where in the modern picture the vehicles are parked in the roadway.

Although the property has been extended, Acors is still recognisable in this 1920s picture. Claud Carpenter was the farmer in those days and he can be seen preparing the milk churn for collection. Hay-making took place in the fields behind the house.

1874.   South Green, Burstead

Fred Spalding
Photo
Chelmsford
Copyright

At the junction with Kennel Lane Hickstars Lane runs down to meet the Southend Road. The 1900 view and that of 1997 are totally different. Chickens wander along the road, the village pump can be seen on the left and the buildings are farm houses. At the junction turn right for South Green.

To the left of Hickstars Lane stood Bridge Cottage (below right)

To the east of Billericay on the Southend Road is South Green. Originally known as Southwoode Green, the village green was clearly shown on the oldest surviving map of Billericay in 1593, although it was properly established hundreds of years prior to that date.

The picture below is of a gang of South Green workmen posing for this picture in Southend Road.

Both the top and middle pictures are of the junction of Grange Road and Southend Road. In the top picture the view is down the Southend Road towards Wickford whilst the middle is down Grange Road. The top photograph was taken in 1909 when the village green was fenced around its perimeter. The sign on the green announces it is the 'South Green Recreation Ground' and there are goal posts erected inside. In the distance can be seen greenhouses. Today the junction is very busy and the layout completely changed from the rural setting.

The sign on the left-hand side of Grange Road advertised the *Plough*, a Mann Crossman and Paulin brewery house. The *Plough* was on the right-hand side of the road and the building is now the doctor's surgery at South Green (white buildings in the modern picture). This property was badly damaged by a bomb during the war and the pub was moved, via temporary accommodation, to its new premises in 1962.

The post office at South Green was within Charles Coe's general provisions store. (The right postcard was posted at South Green on 3 September 1926.)

The picture below is of the Grange Road/Southend Road junction. Grange Parade, a small neighbourhood shopping centre, now exists where cottages and front gardens used to abut Grange Road.

102052.

The road junction at South Green, showing Outwood Lane looking north east; the lane is still a dirt track. The modern picture shows that the area in 1997 is fully developed.

With the development of the motor car the small one-pump South Green garage expanded and, as shown in the left picture, was selling paraffin and diesel in addition to having two petrol pumps. Main Road garage was demolished and replaced in 1991 by a new modern service station.

Going east along the Southend Road, after passing Outwood Common Road, Goodey's Stores (below) were on the left-hand side and opposite the village green. It was a general provisions shop situated next to the garage in the village. The building to the left is the back of the Old Forge, which was behind the garage.

Mr. Houghton was the South Green village blacksmith. The bottom picture is a splendid record of the village smithy with the blacksmith to the left and the various wagons and wheels for repair on the right. In 1997 the forge is completely built upon and it is impossible to take a comparison photograph.

The *Duke of York* public house is on the Southend Road, 200 metres beyond South Green on the road towards Wickford. There has been a public house on this site since 1823 when a James Wood was the licensee. The property was originally two cottages built *c*.1801. In the publication *The Inns of Billericay* by Wynford P. Grant an interesting, and probably true, suggestion is put forward as to how this public house obtained its name. When England was threatened with invasion by Napoleon, various volunteer groups were formed to defend their neighbourhood. One such group was the Great Burstead Militia which was reviewed at Great Burstead by the then Duke of York. Following the review the pub was named in the duke's honour.

In the picture below a bus, heading towards Billericay, passes the *Duke of York*.

The local hunt passes Southend Farm on the Southend Road (bottom).

The middle picture shows Mr. Cole of the South Green Dairy displaying his produce.

Top is a picture of a gang of reapers who were working at Southend Farm and right is John Argent, a horseman on the same farm.

Past the *Duke of York* on the Southend Road is the *King's Head*. The top picture shows a charabanc parked outside whilst the day trippers to Southend were partaking of a refreshment or two. This public house used to be the *White Horse*, opened after 1750, but by 1760 it had changed its name to the *King's Head*.

In the above picture the perimeter fence of the green is on the left-hand side. On the right in the distance can be seen Main Road garage with its then solitary petrol pump and in the foreground the building of R.J. Hall, newsagent, stationer and tobacconist, who also served teas and ices

Down from Great Burstead Church, Church Street becomes Mill Road, which itself forms a junction with Southend Road as it leads away from South Green. Turning down Mill Road, Grange Farm is on the left. The right picture is of a shooting party at the Grange. The barn in the background is still in existence.

All three pictures are of the same road junction, that of the Southend Road with Harding Elm Road. The three local lads pose for the photographer at the junction of the roads with Billericay and Brentwood to the west, Vange, Pitsea and Bowers Gifford to the south and Wickford and Southend to the east. (The top postcard was posted in Walthamstow on 3 October 1908.) The car in the picture left belongs to the photographer. The 1997 pictures reflects the change time has brought about to this rural road junction.

Just past the Harding Elm Road turnoff and prior to reaching Crays Hill Village the road passes Whitesbridge. (The bottom postcard was posted in Billericay on 10 August 1908.)

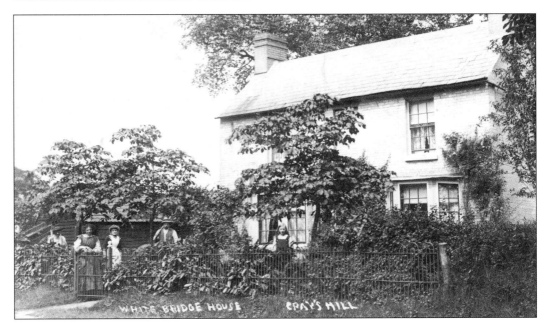

WHITE BRIDGE HOUSE   CRAY'S HILL

The Chase — Crays Hill

Just as you are about to enter the village The Chase (now renamed Oak Avenue) is on the right-hand side. The above picture is undated but is around the 1910s. Only the cottages were in existence on The Chase which led to the entrance of Great Barns. Today the avenue is lined with dwellings but the three cottages remain.

The building to the right in the top postcard (posted in Billericay on 29 May 1909) is Pump Cottage, shown also to the left of the middle postcard. The water for the village would have been supplied by the pump outside Pump Cottage. In the top picture note the water barrel on a cart.

On the curve of the road, just past The Chase, was Crays Hill School. Unfortunately it was demolished many years ago. The view below, dated *c*.1911, shows the Rev. Headmaster overseeing the departing children after the close of school in the afternoon.

Pump Cottage is to the left of the road whilst the school is hidden by the foliage. The modern picture shows the scene today. The entrance to the school was approximately in the middle of the existing modern road.

CRAYS HILL VILLAGE

This turn-of-the-century picture (above) of the centre of Crays Hill village clearly shows the village water supply in the foreground. The dirt road winds its way up the hill with no visible activity at all.

Slightly further up the hill were three timber-framed weather-boarded cottages which remain today. The far cottage was a shop selling refreshments, cigarettes, teas, etc. The coach stop for Southend is on one of the poles from which the Union Jack is flying. It is unfortunate that the sign affixed to the front of the shop cannot be fully deciphered. It declares that the shop is 'The best ? in the village', but what it was best at is unknown!

Opposite the shop and up the hill on the right-hand side was the Crays Hill post office. The early 1900s photograph (top) captures this now demolished building.

The postcard above shows the view of the village looking down Crays Hill, being taken from halfway up. The two young boys have posed for the photographer in the middle of the dirt road. If they tried the same in 1997 they would probably be run over by one of the hundreds of motorcars that use this very busy road.

Crays Hill village provided refreshments to travellers heading further afield. This postcard of Fairview was posted in Billericay on 9 July 1907. The sign on the front fence speaks for itself: 'Crays Hill. The Best House of Call on the Road'.

The entrance to Great Barns is at the end of The Chase. (The left postcard was sent by the then owner on 28 May 1901 and posted in London.) The bottom picture is taken from Crays Hill looking down Rectory Lane. This lane has been renamed and is now known as Church Lane, which leads to St Mary's Church. The building was the rectory but because of the growth of foliage it is impossible to take a similar photograph in 1997.

Nearing the top of Crays Hill, Hope Road is on the right. The view in both pictures is towards Crays Hill and the property on the left in both pictures is one and the same building; the top of the property was removed and the house was converted into a bungalow. (The top postcard was posted in Billericay on 27 August 1911.)

Crays Hill, The Shepherd & Dog.

Over the crest of the hill Crays Hill continues down towards Wickford when it becomes London Road at the Church Road junction for the Ramsdens. At the first bend there is the *Shepherd and Dog* public house on the right-hand side, which was in existence at the turn of the century. Despite the intervening years the scene has hardly changed, though the petrol station has expanded in accordance with the increase of motor traffic.

This 1909 photograph of Idris Ltd.'s five-ton Foden Wagon No.1053 captures the stationary steam machine outside the *Shepherd and Dog* at Crays Hill.

Travelling away from Crays Hill towards Wickford along the London Road, we must turn north at the junction with Church Road in order to reach the Ramsdens. (The postcard below was posted in Wickford on 7 August 1923.) The buildings, which are at the corner of Church Road, are Woolshots Dairy. Notice the farm's truck parked in front of the barn with the wagon to the left of the picture. Although there have been alterations to the buildings, the farm is still in existence. The cottage on the right-hand side of the road has been demolished.

Travelling northwards along Church Road the route traverses the river Crouch. (The postcard of the bridge was posted in Ramsden Heath on 18 July 1910. The later postcard [below] was posted in Billericay on 28 September 1938.)

These postcards reflect the 1920s view of the Ramsden Bellhouse section of Church Road. Many of these bungalows are in existence in 1997. (The right postcard was posted in Ramsden Heath on 10 October 1922 whilst the left card was posted in Poplar, London on 8 August 1925.)

Going towards Ramsden Heath along Church Road, Homestead Road is on the left-hand side. The properties below are on the left-hand side of Homestead Road, travelling away from the junction.

Past Homestead Road, but prior to reaching the railway bridge, is St Mary's Church on the left-hand side. Set in its own large grounds, St Mary's was chiefly rebuilt in 1880 with the exception of the porch and belfry. The porch is *c.*14th-century and the belfry *c.*15th-century. The records and registers of St Mary's date from 1667.

The first passenger steam railway train traversed this bridge on 1 January 1889 when construction of the railway line connecting Wickford with Billericay was completed. The bridge itself was demolished in 1997, being replaced with a modern equivalent, after over 108 years of service. Both the old and modern pictures are facing towards Ramsden Heath.

This early 1900s picture is of the original *Fox & Hounds* public house when it was on Heath Road in Ramsden Heath prior to the transfer of its licence to the new *Fox & Hounds* in 1927. The new public house (as it was then in 1927) is in Church Road only a few yards on the Ramsden Heath side of the railway bridge.

Once the *Fox & Hounds* is left behind, Ramsden Heath is at the end of Church Road where it forms a junction with Downham Road. The top picture, taken *c*.1909, shows Church Road as it approaches the village crossroads. There is a clear view across the fields to Heath Road on the left. The modern picture (left) is evidence of the development of houses along Church Road with the view limited to the shops at the village junction at the end of the road.

The multi-view postcard was posted in Ramsden on 11 October 1931.

RAMSDEN. 1562.

Fred Spalding.
Photo.
Chelmsford.
Copyright.

Post Office, Ramsden Heath.

The top picture is of the north side of Downham Road opposite Church Road and the entrance to the *White Horse* public house. Comparing the modern-day photograph it is difficult to believe that this is the same location. All the original properties appear to have been demolished. The left picture is of the Ramsden Heath post office in Dowsetts Lane opposite the *White Horse*.

These pictures are of the *White Horse* public house looking east with Church Road passing behind the public house in both pictures. (The top postcard was posted in Billericay on 22 March 1913.) The 1997 picture reflects the changes to the scene beyond Church Road. The war memorial was erected to honour the Ramsden men who died in the Great War.

The Cross Roads.
Ramsden Heath.

The top postcard was posted in Ramsden Heath on 4 August 1927. The picture is of the Ramsden Heath Cash Stores and is on the corner of Dowsetts Lane, looking towards Billericay.

The early 1900s picture (middle) is of what is now the Ramsden Heath Free Church, which is on the corner of Heath Road with Park Lane. The property was extended in 1935 and there are a large number of foundation stones in the extension.

The bungalows (bottom) are on the left-hand side of Park Lane looking up towards Heath Road. The two properties in the foreground are still in existence whilst the remainder have been demolished and replaced.

RAMSDEN. 1565.

Fred Spalding.
Photo.
Chelmsford.
Copyright.

Leaving the village centre and after passing Park Lane, St John's Church is on the right-hand side of the road, albeit now hidden by foliage. The church, which is wooden framed and covered entirely with corrugated iron, has a solitary bell and survives today.

Heading west towards Billericay along the Heath Road you will have to look back the way you have travelled for this view. Prior to reaching this point you will pass Chithams on the left and then these properties on the right although they are on the left when looking back towards Ramsden Heath.

The postcard below was posted in Billericay on 16 August 1910 and the properties on the left-hand side can still be seen today.

"Chilhams" Ramsden Heath

Heath Road runs into Norsey Road which eventually forms a junction with the High Street. Prior to reaching Jackson's Lane, Little Norsey Road is on the right (top left).

Jackson's Lane (originally known as Jacksmiths Lane) used to run from Norsey Road to Outwood Common Road (then known as Outwood Lane) near its junction with the Southend Road at South Green. The 1911 view is from the Green Farm Lane section looking south. Development has encroached into the surrounding countryside. (The centre postcard was posted in Epping on 6 June 1911.)

Jackson's Lane used to be a continuous lane from its junction with Norsey Road until it met the Outwood Common Road at South Green. The Sunnymede Estate was developed by a Mr. Edmund Sears after the First World War and the two pictures above were taken from Jackson's Lane; today that section of the lane is now Green Farms Lane. The top picture is a photograph of 'The Meadow Way Stores' which was also the Sunnymede post office. The former dirt track of the 1920s is now a busy back route. (The middle postcard was posted in Billericay on 3 August 1929.)

From Outwood Common Road turn right back on to the Southend Road and Bell Hill returns you to Billericay High Street. At the bottom of the hill used to be Drovers Pond and at the top the Billericay windmill. Drovers Pond (right) was used for the watering of sheep and cattle being driven to market. The two cottages in the foreground, a former beer drinking house, no longer exist but Mill Cottages still do. The modern picture is taken from the point where Drovers Pond used to be. Modern houses now replace the demolished cottages but Mill Cottages can be seen despite the growth of the surrounding trees.

At the top of Bell Hill stood the Billericay windmill. Records suggest that there has been a windmill on or very near this site since 1563. The last miller was William Wood who died in 1866 after which the mill fell into decay. The mill was used in the First World War as an observation post for enemy aircraft. The mill collapsed in 1929 when a severe gale struck Billericay and it was literally blown down. (The postcard left was posted on 14 September 1932.)

The building in the top 1905 picture is of South Lodge on the Southend Road, leading into Billericay, after climbing Bell Hill. As can be seen by the 1997 picture, the property and the large tree in the distance are still there. The road is hardly recognisable today following the construction of a new road which now takes the traffic southwards to Basildon. The dirt track is now a major roundabout dealing with all the traffic coming from Basildon and Wickford.

The picture left is of a wedding car taken at a wedding on 8 July 1916 at South Lodge.

SOUTHEND ROAD, BILLERICAY.

After passing South Lodge, Lockers Hall is on the left. This road forms a junction with Chapel Street and Sun Street, both of which lead back to the High Street. The pictures on this page were taken north of that junction facing southwards. The top photograph was taken at the end of the 19th century. The large tree within the grounds of Lockers Hall can clearly be seen. The property, although hidden in 1997 by foliage, is still in existence, unlike the other property, which could be seen at the end of the road before it turned east.

Arriving back in the High Street brings the 'tour' of Billericay to an end. Unlike this postcard, which was posted in 1914, there are still many undiscovered and inaccessible pictures of Billericay waiting to see the light of day.

Bibliography

Amos, G.S., *A History and Description of the Parish Church of St Mary Magdalen* (1959)

Banks, H.G., *The Basson Family Billericay* (1963)

Brown, A.F.J., *Essex People 1750-1900* (1972)

Carpenter, R.J., *Christopher Martin, Great Burstead and the Mayflower* (1982)

Cox, J.C., *Essex*, Little Guides, 7th edn (1952)

Edwards, A.C., *A History of Essex* (1995)

Fairfull, R., *The Economic Fortunes of Two Essex Market Towns c.1200-1500: A Study of Billericay and Waltham Holy Cross*

Grant, W.P., *The Billericay Reference Book* (1963-4)

Grant, W.P., *The Inns of Billericay*

Grant, W.P., *The Mills of Billericay*

Grant, W.P., *A Short History of Billericay*

Grant, W.P., *Billericay & The Mayflower & The Place Names of Billericay*, 2nd edn (1966)

Grant, W.P., *Billericay Markets and Fairs and the Story of Norsey Wood*

Harper, W.G., *Billericay Through The Ages* (1973)

McKenzie, G., *Thoughts on Billericay* (1989)

McPherson, Murdoch, Webb and Ward, *South Green: A Short History* (1995)

Meecham and Proctor, *Billericay in Old Postcards* (1985)

Neale, K., *Essex in History* (1977, 1997)

Needham, Miss M., *Billericay at the Outbreak of the First World War* (1993)

Morant, P., *The History and Antiquities of the County of Essex* (1763-8)

Morris, J. (ed.), *Domesday Book: Essex* (1983)

Pevsner, N., *The Buildings of England: Essex* (1954)

Reaney, P.H., *The Place Names of Essex* (1935)

Richman H., *Billericay and its High Street* (1953, 1963)

Royal Commission on Historical Monuments, *Historical Monuments in Essex* (1923)

Tait, C.G., *The Parish Churches of South West Essex* (1995)

Walker, G., *The History of a Little Town* (1947)

Index